LONDON

The Ultimate London Travel Guide By A Traveler For A Traveler

The Best Travel Tips; Where To Go, What To See And Much More

SECOND EDITION

Table of Contents

Why Lost Travelers Guides?

First, we want to wish you an amazing time in London when you plan to visit. Also we would like to thank you and congratulate you for downloading our travel guide, *"London; The Ultimate London Travel Guide By A Traveler For A Traveler"*.

Allow us to explain our beginnings, and the reason we created Lost Travelers. Lost Travelers was created due to one simple problem that other guides on the market did not solve; loss of time. Considering it's the 21st century and everything is available online, why do we still purchase guidebooks? To save us time! That's right.

Since the goal is to be efficient and save time, we did not understand why there are several guidebooks on the market that are of 500 to 1000 page' long. We do not believe one needs that much bluff to get an overview of the location and some remarkable suggestions. Considering many guidebooks on the market are filled with "suggestions" that were sponsored for, we have decided to take a different approach and provide our travelers with an honest opinion and decline any sort of sponsorship. This simply allows us to cut off any nonsense and create our guides the Lost Travelers style.

Our mission is simple; to create an easy to follow guide book that outlines the best of activities to do in our limited time at the destination. This easily saves you your most valuable asset; your time. You no longer need to spend hours looking through a massive book, or spend hours searching for information on the internet as we have completed the whole process for you. The best part is we provide you our e-guides for one third the price of the leading brand, and our paper copy for only half the price.

Thanks again for choosing us, we hope you enjoy!

Chapter 1: London at a Glance

London, Great Britain's glamorous capital, stands as one of the world's major hubs of finance, arts, fashion and overall entertainment. The city's history is traceable back to the Roman times, with such notable figures of history such as William the Conqueror having their lives shaped in one way or the other by the city. The truth is that, whether you realize it or not, London has shaped your destiny in one-way or the other. London, being the huge city that it is, is inexhaustible- you could spend months touring it and still get to barely know it. There is perhaps no city in the world that has such a wide variety of people, all living in such deep-seated harmony.

This diversity is what makes London something of an uncut diamond- if you approach it from a differing angle each time, it will present itself in a completely fresh color and shape. From the famous stories associated with it to the distinct high style, London manages to be multiple things in every passing moment.

Chapter 2: Now And Then: The History Of London

For starters, it must be taken into account, to comprehend London's history as well as that of the entire country, that River Thames is the longest river in all of Great Britain, and that for hundreds of years; it was the spine that held London up and nourished it with consistency. Let's now take the journey down London's history lane.

Roman London (1st to 5th Centuries)

London initially came about as a Roman settlement, back in 50 AD. Initially, all Roman London was, was a temporarily set up river base. However, Londinium, as the Romans called it, flourished, becoming the capital of the Roman Empire's Northern most provinces. Along with the usual Roman structures (baths, gardens and temples), they built a sturdy wall around their city to protect it from warring nations.

Anglo-Saxon London (6th to 11th centuries)

The Romans eventually abandoned the city, but given that it was strategically positioned at the banks of the Thames, it meant that the city would not be deserted for too long. Thus, the Vikings and Saxons struggled against each other to gain control of the city, given that its placement was very important, at least from the standpoint of a trade situation. The struggle meant that many parts of the city were destroyed.

This era's most notable figure with regard to the city is the Saxon king, Edward the Confessor. Roughly, a thousand years after the Romans first arrived; he erected his own palace as well as monastery at the riverside, effectively giving London the status of country capital.

The Norman & Medieval London (12th to 15th Centuries)

After Edward died, his cousin, Duke William of Normandy, got a hold of the throne and subsequently, the French, the Normans, invaded England.

In 1066, Duke William started to build the tower of London, in a bid to control the merchants of the city as well as Westminster Hall. As the years passed, other Norman Kings built London bridge as well as multiple churches both within and without of the erected walls.

Tudor London (1485 to 1603)

In this era, London established itself as the capital of what would become a humongous empire. It has been documented that the Tudor King, Henry VIII, separated from the Roman church and founded Anglicanism to be able to marry again and thus, sire a male descendant to take over the reins of the throne. He married 6 times.

It was also at this time that William Shakespeare lived.

19th Century London

During this time, London became the largest city in the world. It also emerged as a global, financial, political, and trading capital. In this unique position, it was unrivalled, at least largely, until the latter part of the 19th Century when both New York and Paris rose up to challenge its dominance.

20th Century & Present London

London entered the 20th century at the height of its influence, as the capital of what was the largest empire in the history of man. The new century was to bring about many things however, like the world wars for instance.

In the year 2005, London won the bid to act as host for the 2012 Olympics, something it did with much success.

Now that you know how London has been throughout the years, let's now put our focus on something else and this is its geography.

Chapter 3: Understanding London: Brief Geographical Stats Of London

As Britain's largest metropolis, it also doubles up as the hub of the country's economy, transportation and culture. London is located in Southeastern England, lying along the River Thames about 50 miles upstream from its North Sea estuary. Looking at satellite imagery, the metropolis is viewed as sitting in compact fashion, in an open land Green Belt. Its principal ring highway (the M25 motorway), is threaded round it at a 20 mile radius from the city center.

Rivers and canals

The River Thames is the largest river in London, and it flows in a west-to-east direction across the London basin.

Within the city, a considerably large number of streams and rivers flow into the River Thames, some of them being large enough to have effectively exerted a significant influence on the area's geography. Many of the smaller-sized London tributaries now primarily flow underground.

Canals

Several canals or canalized rivers have been constructed in the area. The construction, however, was mostly conducted in the 18th and 19th centuries. Originally, the canalized rivers were mainly for trade and goods transportation, all of which have ceased since then. Most of the canals have been preserved but the role they play is mainly leisure based and has a lot to do with tourism.

Topography

At the largest scale, London lies within the London basin bowl. The basin's center is dominated by the Thames' modern valley.

There are a few hills of note, in Greater London, but none of them are any more than a few hundred feet high. Simply put, London takes on a rough circular shape, given that these hills have done little to impede the development of the city in every direction.

The City

The hills present in the City of London, from west to east, have been presumed to have influenced the precise setting of the early city. However, they are minor and as it goes, most of central London is generally flat.

North London

Much of East and Northeast London is situated on a modern floodplain of River Thames.

The Southwest London lower terraces (of the Thames, for specifics), halt suddenly at a bluff that is cut into the London clay and runs south from the Richmond Hill. Clay gate beds randomly cap the higher ground, at least to the east. This combines as with the older Thames gravels that have been dissected by the Beverly Brook valley. This all makes for great viewing, especially for the more technical kind of tourist.

Chapter 4: Where To Stay In London

The overview

London is quite big, as a city, and this means that there are multiple places for you to choose to spend your touring days in. However, there are those that will be more suitable than others especially depending on your budget, since this ultimately determines the nature of services that you can expect. This particular chapter provides you with some of the different areas and the hotels you can expect in them, as you can spend your touring days in. You will also find information on some tourist attractions within the respective areas.

London Central: Paddington, Hyde Park and Bayswater

The neighborhood: Bayswater is located in West London, and it is not to be confused with West End theatre district, that is located just west of the city. It is an attractive residential area, with a collection of stately looking homes as well as several foreign embassies. The Queensway and Bayswater Tube stations are conveniently located just a brief ride to most of London's top attractions. If, for instance, you have the intention to tour Buckingham palace, it will only take you a very short time via tube. However, travel by tube will call for you to build up some mastery of the underground mysteries.

You can find some of the most popular hotels around the area from Booking.com, Ebookers.com or Wotif.com.

What attractions are situated in the neighborhood? Here are some of the most popular attractions around the area:

Royal Albert Hall

The Royal Albert Hall is situated on the northern fringes of South Kensington and is well known for hosting the Proms, a classical music concert, during the summer period since 1941. This spectacular concert hall was opened by Queen Victoria in 1871 and was named after her husband, prince Albert.

Seating up to 5,272 people, the Royal Albert Hall is synonymous with spectacular performances. Leading artists in a wide variety of genres have played here over the decades, hosting some of the most important British events including ballet, opera, contemporary pop, rock, classical, award presentations, charity events and school events. The Royal Albert Hall is a registered charity and holds up to 400 performances each year in the principal hall and an additional 400 in the other areas available.

Initially, the Royal Albert Hall was meant to be named the Central Hall of Arts and Sciences but when Queen Victoria laid the foundation stone in 1867, it was renamed the Royal Albert Hall of Arts and Sciences, in honor of her late husband, who died in 1861.

Albert Memorial

The Albert Memorial is located within Hyde Park just opposite the Albert Hall. It was commissioned in honor of Prince

Albert, the late husband of Queen Victoria. Costing £120,000, it was designed by Sir Gilbert Scott. It is made from bronze gilt and depicts the late prince and is protected by a Gothic canopy. Surrounding him are four statues designed by other notable artists; America by John Bell, Europe by Macdowell, Africa by Theed and Asia by Foley. As you wander around, you will see another group of statues by other artists. Close to the basement there are stunning works by Armstead.

The Albert Memorial is undoubtedly one of the most awe-inspiring monuments within London. Prince Albert was considered virtuous, kind and intelligent, and the erection of such a monument was considered appropriate to him. It stands a testament to his morals and ethics and how he strived for British progression in numerous ways.

Kensington Palace

Kensington Palace is one of several imperial residences in and around London. Located within Kensington Gardens within the Royal Borough, it has been the home of the British royal family since the 17th century. Today, it is the official home of several members of the royal family including Prince William, the Duchess of Cambridge and their children, as well as Prince Harry.

Kensington Palace is a popular destination for domestic and international visitors who come to view the stunningly beautiful State Rooms. They are managed by the non-profit organization, the Historic Royal Palaces. There are numerous objects on display that relate to the history of the British royal family, in addition to a number of beautiful artworks and paintings that belong to the Royal Collection. The grounds are charming and makes for an interesting insight into how much the British people love the monarchy.

Model Museum

The London Toy and Model Museum takes visitors on a fascinating journey through the history of toys and toy-making throughout the centuries. The museum boasts various exhibitions featuring antique toys which still work, as well as those that no longer do and range from cars, trains, airplanes, and plenty of teddy bears. A firm favorite with children and adults alike, the miniature funfairs and train rides are the highlights here. Open seven days a week, it costs around £5.50 for adults and features a variety of temporary exhibitions throughout the year.

Central-Baker Street and Marylebone

The neighborhood: It is a very busy neighborhood, as well as a solid place to stay if at all you are on a tight budget. Paddington is well served by tube stations in Bayswater, Paddington, Lncaster Gate, Queensway and Marble Arch. There are no major tourist attractions present in Paddington. However, there is a nearby attraction at Hyde Park. You can check nearby hotels from Hotels.uk, 1-click.net, Booking.com, or Kayak.co.uk.

Knightsbridge, High Street Kensington

The neighborhood: Knightsbridge is practically next door to South Kensington, and one of the traits that make it an attractive place for the tourist is that it is home to Harrods, the icon of shopping in London. If you stay here, you will have easy tube rides to Green Park, Piccaddily Circus, Covent Gardens, and Leicester Square. You can check out some of the popular hotels around the area from Booking.com, Hoteldirect.co.uk, or Room4u.org.uk.

Attractions in the neighborhood

Harrods

Harrods is the crème de la crème of shopping, whether in London or the rest of the world. The luxury shopping store can be found on Brompton Road in Knightsbridge. The store is spread over several floors featuring 330 departments over 90,000 square meters. Visitors are advised that there is a strict dress code – if you are wearing sneakers than you won't be able to enter. One of the best times to visit Harrods is at Christmas, when the Christmas department opens and creates an indoor Winter Wonderland.

Wellington Arch

The wellington Monument was erected in honor of Arthur Wellesley, who is better known as the First Duke of Wellington, and his military achievements during the Peninsular War and the latter part of the Napoleonic Wars.

The monument can be found on Park Lake and was instated on the 18th June 1822. Standing at 36 feet tall, it is an imposing statue dedicated to one of Britain's greatest heroes.

Upon the base of the monument sits at 18 foot tall statue of Achilles, the legendary Trojan hero from Greek mythology. It was designed by Richard Westmacott from the melted down cannons which belonged to Britain's enemies. The statue shows Achilles as a highly toned nude man, brandishing a sword in his right hand while lifting a shield in the other. His armor rests against his right thigh, his cloak covering his left shoulder.

The funds for the Wellington Monument were raised by British women, who raised £10,000. What makes this monument really interesting is that since the Roman period, it was the first nude statue to be erected in London, even if there was a fig leaf over his genitals, it still created a bit of an uproar amongst the people.

Hyde Park

If there is one park you should visit while in London, then make sure it is Hyde Park. Hyde Park is one of the biggest in the city and one of the royal parks, one of four that create a link from Kensington Palace to Hyde Park. It goes past Buckingham Palace, separated by the Serpentine, and going through St. James Park.

Hyde Park is often considered to be part of Kensington Gardens, although this is a misconception. The two parks used to be one, but they were divided by Queen Caroline in 1728. Hyde Park is spread out over an area of 142 hectares or 350 acres, while Kensington Gardens measures at 111 hectares, or 275 acres. If the two are put together, they are actually bigger than Monaco.

Hyde Park features a number of attractions, including the Princess Diana monument, Serpentine Lake, and the Speaker's Corner. It opens around 5am and remains open until around midnight. Throughout the year, the park hosts a number of events and performances. Not only is it home to various cultural attractions, visitors will find the Royal Parks Foundation Education Centre and is a fantastic place to spot various wildlife scampering around.

Natural History Museum

London is famous for its multitude of museums but the Natural History Museum located in South Kensington, is certainly one of the best. Dedicated to the understanding and continued education of natural history, it is one of three museums situated on the same road – the others being the Victoria and Albert Museum and the Science Museum.

Inside, there is an abundance of artifacts and specimens to marvel at – 80,000,000 of them to be exact. Spread out over five principal collections – paleontology, zoology, botany, mineralogy and entomology – the museum boasts a reputation as a leading educational center for taxonomy and conservation. One of the highlights of the Natural History Museum includes the Charles Darwin collection, featuring a range of specimens the famous explorer discovered and brought back.

The paleontology collection is one of the best in Europe, featuring a variety of dinosaur skeletons, the main one being the gigantic diplodocus skeleton which overwhelms the main hall. In addition to the dinosaur collection, the museum is renowned for its library. Containing an extensive collection of books, journals and other literary works, visitors can only access the library by appointment.

Mayfair, Park Lane and Oxford Street

The neighborhood: Basically, what you have in this area are the "Royal London" hotels. This is purely four as well as five star territory. It is served by several tube stops at Hyde Park Corner, Marble Arch, Green Park, and Oxford Circus. You can check out some hotels from Booking.com, LondonTookKit.com, Oxfordstreet.co.uk, Hoteldirect.co.uk or Expedia.com.

Attractions in the neighborhood:

Buckingham Palace

Buckingham Palace is one of the top attractions in London. It is the official residence and the administrative center for Queen Elizabeth, the reigning monarch of the United Kingdom. The imposing building is located within Westminster and regularly holds state occasions, receiving royal and diplomatic visitors from all over the world.

While it is the Queen's palace today, the building was originally known as Buckingham House. The main center of the palace was a beautiful townhouse which was constructed in 1703 for the Duke of Buckingham, the land upon which it stands being in private hands for over 150 years. In 1761, King George III attained Buckingham House and gave it to Queen Charlotte, upon which it was known as the Queen's House. During the 1800s, the building underwent enlargement by John Nash and Edward Blore, renowned architects, who designed an additional three wings and the main courtyard. In 1837, it became the official monarch's residence when Queen Victoria took the throne.

Piccadily Circus

Located in London's West End in Westminster, Piccadilly Circus is a public area which was established in 1819 to join Piccadilly with Regent Street. The 'circus' part of the name is taken from the Latin word which means circle.

Piccadilly is a great place if you want to experience London at its busiest and most energetic. Within close distance are the theatres located on Shaftesbury Avenue, the Haymarket, Glasshouse Street and Coventry Street. There are a wide variety of bars, restaurants, shopping centers, clubs and other entertainment venues within the area. Piccadilly Circus is famous for its bright neon lights, its video display system and the Shaftesbury Memorial Fountain and Statue (and no, it's not of Eros, even though it looks like him). There are a number of famous buildings here including the London Pavilion and the Criterion Theatre.

Bond Street

Bond Street is one of the most famous shopping streets in London. Located within London's prestigious West End, it joins up with Piccadilly to the south and Oxford Street to the north. Since the 18th century, Bond Street has been the home to numerous renowned luxury stores and brands, selling everything from fashion wear to jewelry and high class goods. The southern part is known as the Old Bond Street, and the extended part in the north is the New Bond Street, but not many people will use these distinctions in day to day life.

Bond Street was first constructed on the fields which surrounded Clarendon House in Piccadilly, constructed by Sir Thomas Bond. During the early 18th century, the street was extended and expanded and by the late 18th century, it was frequented by Mayfair's social elite who would come to socialize. Although numerous designed and luxury stores were added, the social aspect of the street deteriorated but still retained its reputation as one of the best shopping destinations in the city. Today, there are a number of designer stores to visit including Tiffany's and Fenwick, along with Sotheby's and Bonhams.

Fortnum and Mason

Usually known just as Fortnum's to locals, Fortnum and Mason is a luxury department store located in Piccadilly, with other branches located at Heathrow Airport and Railway Station within the UK in addition to branches in Dubai and other international destinations. Its main branch is located at 181 Piccadilly and was founded in 1707 by William Fortnum and High Mason.

Originally, Fortnum's was a grocery store, with a reputation for providing only the best items. Throughout the Victorian period, they were able to expand into selling a range of other goods, although Fortnum's still provides fresh, exotic and specialty food items. Come here to browse for a range of items before heading upstairs to try some freshly cooked dishes at the numerous restaurants or the Tea Shop. The Gentleman's department is located on the third floor, the perfect place to spoil the man in your life.

The National Portrait Gallery

Also known as the NPG, the National Portrait Gallery is one of London's most distinguished art galleries. Boasting a wonderful collection of portraits depicting British historic celebrities and illustrious individuals, it was the first of its kind worldwide when it first opened in 1856. In 1896, it was transferred to St. Martin's Place, close to Trafalgar Square, adjacent to the National Gallery. Since then, it has been enlarged two times with other branches throughout the country.

The gallery showcases portraits of some of Britain's most famous and important figures throughout history. The paintings are done by a variety of artists, some better known than others. Not only can you see paintings, but the National Portrait Gallery also houses a fantastic collection of drawings, photographs and sculptures. The highlight of the National Portrait Gallery is the Chandos portrait, which depicts the famous British playwright, William Shakespeare, although there are theories which claim the image isn't of him.

Earls Court and Hammersmith

The neighborhood: There are numerous cost-friendly hotels in this area, as well as bookstores and restaurants. As it goes, it is an incredibly busy conventional area, with easy access by tube. You can check out popular hotels around the area from Booking.com or Tripadvisor.com

Neighborhood attractions

The Natural History Museum

London is famous for its multitude of museums but the Natural History Museum located in South Kensington, is certainly one of the best. Dedicated to the understanding and continued education of natural history, it is one of three museums situated on the same road – the others being the Victoria and Albert Museum and the Science Museum.

Inside, there is an abundance of artifacts and specimens to marvel at – 80,000,000 of them to be exact. Spread out over five principal collections – paleontology, zoology, botany, mineralogy and entomology – the museum boasts a reputation as a leading educational center for taxonomy and conservation. One of the highlights of the Natural History Museum includes the Charles Darwin collection, featuring a range of specimens the famous explorer discovered and brought back.

The paleontology collection is one of the best in Europe, featuring a variety of dinosaur skeletons, the main one being the gigantic diplodocus skeleton which overwhelms the main hall. In addition to the dinosaur collection, the museum is renowned for its library. Containing an extensive collection of books, journals and other literary works, visitors can only access the library by appointment.

Brompton Oratory

Brompton Oratory, or better known as the Church of the Immaculate Heart of Mary, is a Grade II listed building designed in the neo-classical architectural style. Located in Knightsbridge, it's often mistaken as a clergy but is actually a church. It boasts a relationship with the London Oratory School, the funding for the boys' school funded by the priests. Visitors can come here to admire the beautiful architectural design and the artworks housed within, as well as attend mass. You can even pick up a CD at Brompton Oratory of two of their choirs singing.

Kensington Gardens

Kensington Gardens are one of several royal parks found within the city, west of Hyde Park, to which it once belonged to. Spread out over 111 hectares, or 270 acres, they have long been the playground of British royals. During his reign, Henry VIII would chase deer through the gardens. When Kensington Palace was established in 1689, William and Mary created a new park. Mary decided that she would try to make William, who was from Holland, feel welcome in Britain so created a formal garden in a distinctive Dutch style.

In 1702, when Anne became Queen, the gardens were redesigned in a much more British style, with the orangery established two years later. It was designed to safeguard the fragile citrus trees from the cold British weather and later she would entertain here, its delicate beauty ideal when the city was too chaotic.

In the late 1720s, Queen Caroline began redesigning the gardens into what we see today. The Serpentine Lake and the Long Water were added, as well as the broad Walk and the Round pool. However, in the 18th century, the park was only opened to the public on Saturdays and if you weren't suitably dressed then you were not permitted to enter. Today, however, you don't have to worry about dress codes – everyone is welcome to enjoy the park in all its spectacular beauty.

Serpentine Gallery

The Serpentine Galleries are two modern art galleries located within London. Made up of the Serpentine Gallery and the Serpentine Sackler Gallery, they are only a few minutes walk over the bridge from the other. They are named after the Serpentine Lake which they stand beside and see up to 1.2 million visitors throughout the year.

The Serpentine Gallery was founded in 1970 within a Grade II building. The building used to be a tea pavilion constructed in the early 1930s by J. Grey West. Today, the galleries host a variety of exhibitions on art and architecture and enjoy a reputation for education and variety of classes and programs for schools and individuals. Some of the biggest names who have had their works displayed here include Gustav Metzger, Damien Hirst, Andy Warhol, Man Ray and Paula Rego. Since Diana, Princess of Wales, was a patron of the Serpentine Galleries, there is a memorial to the late princess located at the entrance.

Olympia Exhibition centers

The Olympia Exhibition Center, located within West Kensington, is a worldwide renowned exhibition center. Hosting a variety of international trade events and conferences today, it was founded in 1886 by John Whitley as the National Agricultural Hall.

Whitley wanted a place where he could host the biggest indoor show center in the country. Not long after its opening, it was renamed the Olympia Exhibition Hall in reference to the notions surrounding its concept. When the Grand Hall was created, it was said to be the biggest in the country that used one length of glass and iron. Today, the Olympia Exhibition Hall boasts four venues and the conference center, consisting of the Grand Hall, the National Hall, the Central Hall and the West Hall.

Chapter 5: Transport

Get In

Assuming that you take a flight to London, you will land in any of the following 6 main airports namely Heathrow, Gatwick, or Stansted, Southend, Luton, or City.

Heathrow, Stansted and Gatwick airports are all served by dedicated train services. They are also served by the standard commuter services. The Heathrow Express Service, from Paddington, is provided by BAA plc, the airport operator, while the Gatwick Express, from Victoria as well as the Stansted Express from Liverpool Street are all provided by assorted train operating services. Well, this is not all there is about transportation from each of the airports but is a good starting point.

How To Get Around: Transport In London

The overview

The transport network in London is extensive, with the inclusion of both public and private services. Actually, about 25% of all of London's journeys are made via public transport systems. Private journeys account for roughly 41% of all journeys. While this book might not be comprehensive enough for all travel in London, it will give you a quick overview of what to expect.

Transport For London (TfL) is the government body responsible for transportation within the city. The body has a reliable website that can help you plan your journey around the city especially with its Journey Planner. You can call them on ☎ 0843 222 1234 (or text 60835) to ask suggestions on how to move to whichever location you want. The good thing is that TfL has a single ticketing system known as Oyster that can help you to switch travel modes on a single ticket.

To make your travel easy, we will discuss the 2 broad travel options and how to use various modes within these options:

Within Central London

Boat: You can take a boat cruise along River Thames. The boats are privately run but are part of TfL's network.

Tube/Underground: There are 11 color-coded lines that cover the suburbs and the central area

Docklands Light Railway (DLR): This one runs in the east of London to provide links to London City Airport, Stratford, Canary Wharf/Docklands, Greenwich etc. It is privately run but actually part of the TfL's network.

Airport Express: These are rail services operating around the 6 airports. The trains heading to Heathrow are privately operated but those for other airports are part of the UK rail network, beyond the TfL network so you won't be able to use the Oyster card.

Suburban London

National Rail: This one runs a complex suburban network of rail services especially in the southern suburbs although you can still find it in the north. This one is privately operated and not part of the TfL network.

Tram/Tramlink: This operates only within the southern parts especially around Croydon and Wimbledon

Over ground: There are orange colored lines that circle the different northern suburbs to connect Stratford, with Richmond Upon Thames. This is a complex network with many interconnections. Learn more about it here.

Note: Both the DLR and the Underground account for about 40% of the bulk of journeys between inner and Outer London. This makes them the most highly utilized in London.

Ticketing

Usually, London commuters will mostly gain access to the public transport services in London by an inter-modal travel ticket that is provided by Transport for London (TFL). Oyster Card is credit card-sized, offering almost unlimited use for the entire train network services in all of the Greater London area. The tickets, including the Pay As You Go model are actually cost effective for you especially if you intend to do lots of traveling in a day. For instance, it costs about 12 pounds for a full day unlimited travel on London's public transportation. Obviously, if you compare this with having to pay for every bus, tube or train ride, you will notice that you have saved a lot.

Tip: When riding the tube, be sure to touch the reader (touch out) when you get to your destination to avoid being charged extra (a £7.20 charge).

Note: Oyster can also save you time getting into buses since you don't need to queue to use the contactless bank card or the paper travel card. Please note that you cannot pay bus fare on London buses using cash.

To save more money during your travel, you can load your Travelcard onto your Oyster card or purchase a paper ticket for several days:

Unlimited day Travelcard within Zones 1-6 - £12
Unlimited 7 day Travelcard within Zone 1-2 – about £30.40
Unlimited Monthly Travelcard within Zones 1-2 – about £116.08
Unlimited Annual Travelcard within Zones 1-2 – about £1,216.00

You can buy tickets from all tube station ticket offices for use on DLR, London Overground, Tram Service, bus and National Rail. You will need to choose the zones (from 1-9) as you buy the card. If you are traveling outside a chosen zone, use PrePay to save money on travel.

Travelcard is older and is combined with a National Rail Ticket. It will offer the same intermodal access but is valid to use at those regional railroad stations that have not yet been kitted out to offer electronic ticketing.

The London Pass will offer tourists who are visiting London a combination of the Travelcard and admissions to several tourist attractions for an advance fee.

Roads & Buses

There are a hierarchy of roads in London including orbital trunk and major radial and even minor side streets. At the very top level, you have motorways and carriageways, which are all supplemented by urban dual carriageways, several local distributor roads, as well as small local streets.

Note: The reason why the London road network is often so congested is that the bulk of roads in London were laid out before the car was invented.

Cycling

It will serve you well to know, if you are a cycling enthusiast, that over 1 Million Londoners own bicycles. Currently, there are an estimated 480,000 cycle journeys made each day in the capital. Bikes will be available for hire at several docking stations in Central London.

Taxis

Black cabs and Hire cars

The black cab remains a very common sight in London. Taxis present a very safe way of travel, as they are driven by the only cab drivers in the entire world, who have spent a mandatory 3 years learning the city's road network, so as to gain "ample knowledge". You can hail a black cab on the street or hire from a taxicab rank.

Other modes include:

Walking: London is pedestrian friendly so if you feel up to it, you can always take a walk. This especially saves time for short distance travel during peak hours.

Skating: You can skate anywhere except within the City of London District.

Chapter 6: Top Experiences In London

"When a man gets tired of London, he surely must be tired of life as well."
Samuel Johnson, 1777.

There are numerous unique experiences to experience in the city of London. This chapter will cover several, which are immense fun.

Visit <u>the London zoo</u> and get up close to a giraffe

The zoo has over 12,000 animals including tigers, meerkats and gorillas. There is this 4.3 meter tall giraffe who goes by the name of Ellish and most people who visit her are content to watch her stride as elegantly as any model across her paddock. There are several other giraffes here, with the keepers offering a continuous, informative commentary on the giraffes and their traits. If you have the London Pass, you will have free access to the zoo. The <u>ticket costs</u> about 45 pounds on weekdays and 60 pounds per person on weekends.

Enter a superb cinematic fantasy world

In the real world, an extraordinarily good night does not start with court summons. But then again, the <u>Secret Cinema</u> is no ordinary night out. After buying your ticket, you turn up at the location after receiving a cryptic-style email. You are then promptly incarcerated. In a very convincing mock-up jail, a stern-faced officer issues out grey uniforms and the inmates start to explore the dimly lit corridors. Each room has something different awaiting; candle making, psychoanalysis and the like. Oh, and you can buy beer in brown paper bags from corrupt guards. You can buy tickets here.

Stay at the <u>Hampton Court Palace</u>
According to those that have had the pleasure of <u>visiting the palace</u>, the atmosphere is incredibly warm. Here is what one housekeeper had to say, "The rich past seems to almost ooze out from the neat brickwork."

Sleep in a boat that is perched at the top of Southbank center

The placement of the boat looks as though a freak tsunami caught it and hurled it onto the top of Southbank center where by good luck; it managed to land right side up. The fact though, is that it is there by design, a one-bedroom installation that is complete with a kitchenette and a library that is available to rent out for the night. Inside it are more surprises, ranging from a cabinet of old maps to a logbook that you can fill out, detailing your unique experiences. You will part with about 440-pounds to experience this but this is quite reasonable given the uniqueness of the place.

Get to learn the art of fixing a martini from none other than James Bond

<u>Dukes Bar, in St. James</u> has the unique feel of a gentleman's club. It was also the favorite place of one Ian Fleming, the man who invented James Bond. Here is some interesting history- when Fleming was writing his Bond books in the 50s,

observing impeccable etiquette was a way of showing individual class. For instance, a cocktail was supposed to be stirred, and not shaken, so that the drink would not be murky and full of ice cubes. Thus, when Bond asks for his martini "shaken and not stirred", it is pretty much a statement that this fellow can do whatever he wants.

Here are some other top things you must do:

Watch a movie at any of the many cinemas around the West End, London. The cinemas are especially busy during summer months.

Watch a football match featuring any of the top 5 Premier League clubs namely Arsenal, Tottenham Hotspur, Crystal Place, West Ham United and Chelsea. There are also other football clubs just below that i.e. in the Football League Championship and other lower ranks.

Winter skate for £10-12 (adults)

Summer skate in Mayfair-Marylebone and South West London

Take part in the famous London Pub Quiz

Take a trip through tie at Dennis Severs' House in Spitalfields.

Located in London is the grand 18th century townhouse which belonged to Dennis Severs. It's a beautiful example of Georgian and Victorian era architecture, with each room taking you through a different part of these eras. The family it once belonged to were renowned Huguenot silk weavers; learn more about the history of these periods, and the family themselves, as you wander around the historic building.

Climb the Westminster Cathedral Bell Tower

Do not mistake Westminster Cathedral with Westminster Abbey as so many visitors have done in the past – although it's very easy to di. Westminster Cathedral is an imposing building, it's iconic Byzantine architectural styling standing out. Visitors can make their way up the 83 meter high bell tower and gaze out over the London skyline, the views both impressive and relaxing.

Speak your mind at Speaker's Corner in Hyde Park

For a long time, people have been making their way on Sundays to a section of Hyde Park known as Speaker's Corner in order to inspire people around them by using words. Since 1872, people have had permission to talk about anything you want but don't use any bad language!

Reflect in Highgate Cemetery in Highgate

It might sound a little morbid to visit a cemetery but Highgate Cemetery is unlike any other cemeteries you may come across. This Grade I listed cemetery was established in the Victorian era, where several notable individuals have been laid to rest over the decades. Some of its famous residents include Karl Marx and Beryl Bainbridge. With ivy spreading over the ironwork, Highgate Cemetery captures the eyes and the imagination.

Indulge your inner child at the Little Angel Theatre

Located in Islington, the Little Angel Theatre is really aimed at kids but adults themselves will fall in love with the darling and creative puppet shows the theatre hosts. Be entertained – with or without your own kids – or learn the art of puppetry through the clubs and workshops the theatre hosts throughout the year.

Pay a Visit to Willow Road

Call on 2 Willow Road, Hampstead Heath, and wander around a beautiful 1930s house. Why is it so important? Well, 2 Willow Road was designed by Erno Goldfinger, an architect from Hungry who created many of the familiar features modern houses boast today. As a result, 2 Willow Road was a ground pioneering property and offers tours to those interested in the history of architecture. The property also features a collection of works done by several important figures, including Henry Moore.

Pay a visit to the Bank of England

Paying a visit to the bank may seem a little strange – especially if you're not putting anything in or taking anything out – but the Bank of England is a British institution all on its own. Located in the financial district, the museum takes you on a fascinating journey through what goes on at the bank. The highlight of the museum though is the small gold bar that you can actually lift by yourself.

Hold your breath in horror at the Old Operating Theatre Museum

Situated near London Bridge, the Old Operating Theatre Museum is a small museum not really known to many but it's certainly one that you'll remember. It was here around 150 years ago that Victorian doctors would attempt to save lives by performing surgeries in poor conditions and without anesthetic. Learn more about the ways doctors would amputate infected limbs with a knife or saws.

Surround yourself with flowers at Columbia Road Flower Market

Located in Bethnal Green, the Columbia Road Flower Market blooms into a kaleidoscope of colors and scents on Sundays. Make time to smell the roses – and tulips, lilies and every other kind of flowers of display – and take a bunch home with you.

Go hunting at a car boot sale

There is a multitude of car boot sales all around London that visitors can experience. Usually held at the weekends, visitors can go hunting for bargains and enjoy the atmosphere. Don't forget your haggling skills!

Take a trip to the future at New London Architecture

While London is known for its long, rich history, it's also a city looking to the future. Visitors can join in the discussions of future architecture at the New London Architecture. The gallery also includes the Pipers Central London Model, where designers have created a stunning miniature model of buildings that are due to be constructed.

Chapter 7: Top Cultural Experiences In London

Visit the British Library

The unique thing about the British Library is that every publication produced in both the UK and Ireland is mailed off to the British Library. As you may expect, this institute has amassed a bulk of over 150 million items. Every year, it is the recipient of more than 3 million fresh items. It is possible to apply for access to the reading rooms, or you can simply explore both the permanent and temporary exhibits present in the John Ritblat Gallery. Here, you will find some of the most famous written as well as printed items in the entire world. Here are a few examples- Shakespeare's first folio, the Gutenberg Bible and Handel's Messiah.

Discover Winston Churchill's war rooms

Basically, the Churchill war rooms are purely dedicated to the life and achievements of the former prime minister of Britain, Winston Churchill. There are multiple artifacts on his career in politics, as well as many of his trademark props. Worthy inclusions are his siren suits and a cigar. Less known displays are relative to his occupations as a soldier, journalist, and painter. He was an immensely talented amateur painter who enjoyed going to the races immensely. Original film footage as well as stark photos are displayed in innovative fashion along with a 50 foot, Churchill-themed computerized timeline.

Join the first Thursday's tour

Late night openings as well as events in galleries and museums all over East London usually take place on the first Thursday of every month.

Wander the Horniman Museum

This is an anthropological museum set in about 16 acres of landscaped gardens. It has a rich traditional history gallery, dominated by a very bizarre, stuffed walrus. All the exhibits are displayed in traditional cases with no computerized screens anywhere in sight. This museum provides many family facilities, with the inclusion of a nature trail, a hands-on base, and weekend workshops.

Scream at the Old Operating theatre Museum

This is Britain's oldest operating theatre. It is located in a herb garret, in the roof of a St. Thomas church. Originally built in 1821 for use by poor women, it has been restored with original equipment and furnishings. This is with the inclusion of a 19th century operating table, athological specimens and surgical tools. Visitors gain entry via a wooden staircase to view a non-anesthetic operating theatre. Temporary exhibitions also take place, often combining art with pathological explorations.

Visit the Royal Opera House

Having successfully secured its position as one of the globe's great opera houses, the Royal Opera House has been able to launch something of a PR campaign. In a bold move to draw in audiences, Don Giovanni opening performance of 2008 was made to be exclusive to Sun readers at low rates and then beamed live to a chain of cinemas. Now, you may be a Liverpool fan and thus, full of aversion for the sun, but this should not keep you away from the opera house, which is full of solid experiences.

Chapter 8: Culinary Adventure: The Top Places To Experience Art Of Feasting In London

For a very long time, we have held London as the capital of all things culinary. If you love food, the street food array in London will do more than just impress you. Fun events, food markets in London and even London's finest night markets are bustling with stalls that serve incredible food in disposable containers. Here are some food markets that boast of foods you seriously have to try when you visit London.

The Berwick Street Market

This soho market has all the makings of an historic market. Notable highlights here include <u>Tongue n cheek</u> and <u>Bahn Mi 11</u>. This one is open from Monday to Friday. You can sample fruit scoops and vegetables that are on sale.

Piccadilly good food market

This is open on Mondays, from 11 am to 2 pm. This one is small but immensely reliable with impressive Christopher Wren themed surroundings. There are <u>10 stalls</u>, at most, though these tend to drop to 8 every now and then.

Victoria Good Food Market

This one is open on Thursdays, as from 11 am to 12 pm. Perhaps, the most remarkable thing about the food you find here is that it is not entirely street food. It is half street food, half artisan food. You will find roughly 20 hot food stalls. The cold foods, cakes, and deli goods may be found in the undercover parts. The selection is regularly changing, with Brazilian, Indian, Chinese, Thai, Italian, and Polish foods present. However if you simply want fish and chips, you will not be disappointed either.

The Exmouth Market

This one is open from Monday to Friday from midday to 3 pm. This weekday market is a favorite for the office workers who are based in the area, and it adds to the foodie credentials that are already in place thanks to the multiple restaurants already flanking the street.

Kerb at Gherkin

This is open on Thursdays, as from midday to 2 pm.

Leather Lane Market

Open from Monday to Friday, as from 11 am to 3 pm. You should expect queues especially over the lunch hour.

Chapter 9: Nature & Adventure: The Top Must-Visit Places In London

One of the top reasons why visitors adore touring London is because of the vast array of activities to take part in and the places available to visit. Whatever passions you have, you can be sure that you won't be short of options when you want to tour the city.

The ArcelorMittal Orbit

This is officially one of London's newest attractions, and it has swiftly and steadily risen to become one of the most impressive and iconic places to pay a visit to. The curious structure, as well as the spectacular views over London, are just a few reasons why tourists are so keen on it. With a couple of observation platforms, visitors are able to overlook the Olympic Park, which successfully hosted the 2012 Olympic games. In the summer, there is even a bar hosted at the orbit, allowing you to catch the beautiful sunset with a drink in hand. This, it goes without needing too much explanation, is one of the best ways to spend a long evening.

Attractions along the Thames

You cannot visit London and fail to experience some of the best attractions along its magnificent river, The Thames. The river is surrounded by lots of attractions including but not limited to historic royal palaces, various thrill themed parks and a lot more. Here is a list of some popular attractions that you don't want to miss:

If you are visiting during a cold month, don't forget to explore the royal castle and the historic museum along the river. And if the months are a bit warm, you can check out the gardens, enjoy bird watching and even check out the nature reserve along the river. Also, ensure to visit Oxford, Windsor, and Abingdon since these are rich in history that will teach you a lot.

- Some of the famous gardens along the river include Alexandra gardens, Cliveden, RHS Garden Wisley, The Walled Garden, The Living Rainforest, Stowe, Grey's Court Garden, Friars Court etc.

- If historic buildings or structures tickle your fancy, you can expect to see: Buscot Park, The Vyne, Chastleton House, Sulgrave Manor, Kelmscott Manor, Blenheim Palace, Maharajahs Well, Basildon Park, Buscot Old Parsonage, Fawley Court Historic House & Museum, Stonor Park, Nuffield Place, Kingston Bagpuize House & Garden etc

- If you love nature, you will definitely enjoy the RHS Chelsea Flower Show, held 4 times a year. Additionally, you shouldn't shy away from checking out the Royal Botanical Gardens at Kew and the famous WWT London Wetland Center. And if you have kids, don't fail to visit the Battersea Park and Children's Zoo.

You should also try to attend any of the events held along the River Thames including music, sporting, etc. One of the notable ones in 2015 is the Totally Thames event. Others include Virgin Money London Marathon, BNY Mellon boat race, The Great River Race, and The Mayor's New Year's Eve fireworks display.

Other things you can do along the river include boating, taking a bike tour (including speedboat tours), going on a Thames river cruise, or simply taking a walking tour along the river.

Additionally, don't forget to sample the culture along the river from art, film, and dance to music, theatre etc.; you will get it all. Some of the notable places of culture include Tate Modern, Tate Britain, Shakespeare's Globe Theatre, Southbank Center, BFI Southbank, and National Theatre.

You can also learn a lot about London's past as you move along the river. For instance, you will learn about the HMS Belfast, Royal Museums Greenwich, Tower of London, Houses of Parliament, Hampton Court Palace etc.

If it gets dark while still touring the Thames, don't worry; there are plenty of bars and nightclubs along the river. And if you want to eat, the number of restaurants around the area is also high. Some notable restaurants include The Bingham, Oxo Tower, Perkin Reveller etc. You could even dine while on board the Thames dinner cruise.

Aerial View of London

And if you are tired of exploring London on land, don't forget to ride the Coca Cola London Eye. You cannot afford not to visit the London Eye, which boasts of being the largest observation wheel in the world standing at 135 meters right over London's Southbank. The wheel rotates every 30 minutes. To ride, it will cost £23 per person.

Another notable feature is the famous <u>Shard</u>, which has an <u>observation platform</u> at the 72nd floor making it provide a 40-mile aerial view of the city. It will cost about £25 to get to the platform. A subsequent <u>visit</u> is free if bad weather ruined your first visit. This one is situated in London Bridge.

You can also get aerial views of London by visiting <u>The Monument</u>, which was built after the Great Fire of London in 1666. <u>The Monument</u> is 62m high and has 311 steps up to give you the much-anticipated view of the city of London. Although not as high as the London Eye or the Shard, it is definitely worth visiting. You only pay £3.

When you combine the trip with the Emirates Air Line Cable Car and a quick journey on the famous Thames Clipper, you can bet that you will have an unforgettable experience. Up at The O2 is also a good option to give you a perfect and fairly different aerial view of London. And if money is not really a problem, you should take the London Helicopter tour, which usually flies just above the water to give you a completely new perspective as you tour the city.

Be sure to check out The Gherkin or 30 St Mary Axe, which stands at 180m and provides a great 360-degree aerial view of London from its 40th floor.

Get to learn about various London's bridges

As you move along the river, you will come across different bridges each of which has a long story to tell. It is best to visit the Tower Bridge Exhibition to learn more about the bridges as you move along the river. Some of the notable bridges that you might want to check out include Millennium Bridge, Hungerford Bridge, Albert Bridge etc. You can learn a few things about the bridges here.

The Royal Botanical Kew gardens

Walk around the 120 acres or so of exotic oases in this quiet and rural West London place. Especially if you are staying in the inner city with all its bustle, you will discover that the break it gives you from all the noise and movement is beyond refreshing. Climb up the treetop walk as well as via the Nature Trails and you will experience firsthand just why the Kew Gardens are a must-visit.

Chapter 10: Other Major Attractions In London

Sir John Soane's Museum

This is the former residence of Sir John Soane, the architect of the Bank of England. It is one of the finest public museums in all of London. It has over 20,000 architectural drawings as well as antiquities, with the inclusion of the Egyptian sarcophagus of Seti. The remarkable thing is that the Sarcophagus sits alongside works by the likes of Canaletto, Turner, and Piranesi. Only at this museum can you get this.

The Path of Thames

The Thames is home to lots of London's heralded treasures, with most of them in plain view. The Thames Path however is not so, and its 40-mile long entity has multiple spots to be found out. The best way to tour is to hire a bike, which is relatively easy, and ride the entire way. There will be public beaches, pubs to recharge and Rotherhithe village, which is one of the highlights.

Big Ben

Big Ben is actually a nickname for The Great Bell of the Clock, which is located at the very north side of Palace of Westminster in London. It is also referred to as the clock tower or the Elizabeth Tower (from 2012). This tower prides in having the 2nd largest 4-faced chiming clock in the world. It dates back to 1858 and is undoubtedly one of the symbols of the UK especially when referring to London.

Wilton's Music Hall

This one is a traditional Victorian music hall located in London's Tower Hamlets. In recent years, it has been restored to recapture its former glory. You can book tickets and attend an array of performances or simply drop by for a drink in the very impressive mahogany bar. Or simply, you can take a tour of the wonderful as well as historic venue. Whatever you opt to do; you are guaranteed to have the time of your life.

The Temple

Especially if you are a fanatic of the law, and all things that are based around it, you will want to visit this place. On either side of the Temple Church, you are going to find the inner and middle temple places, all with their own unique gardens, libraries as well as chambers. The Knights Templar established it in the 12th Century and Dan Brown's D Vinci Code borrows heavily from it.

Postman's Park

The unique name came from the popularity that workers in the nearby post office had for it. These days, it is home to the Unique Watts Memorial, which is a vast gallery of glazed tablets detailing various acts of bravery.

Firepower Woolwich

This is located <u>in the Royal Arsenal</u>, on a particularly quiet corner of the River Thames. The museum in Woolwich, during past centuries, was easily one of the most vital munitions manufacture spots, though this was largely kept in secret.

Wallace collection

It is housed in a grand old <u>London Town House, in Marylebone</u>. It mainly displays paintings, porcelain and furniture from 18th century France. In all the 28 rooms, there are works by old masters, with the inclusion of Titan, Rembrandt and Canaletto. The Courtyard Restaurant is, in its own regard, a hidden gem.

Note: London is undoubtedly a large city. You definitely will never be short of options when it comes to places to visit or things to do.

Chapter 11: Best Shopping Areas in London

London is a dream come true for those who love to shop. The city boasts several shopping areas with a reputation for a theme or specialty. You'll discover everything in London – from luxury and designer goods to unusual and vintage objects. With famous luxury department stores such as Harrods, and quirky yet wonderful spots like Portobello Road, London offers something for everyone's budgets and tastes.

Oxford Street

Oxford Street is an iconic part of London's character. Home to over 300 shops and designer outlets, Oxford Street is one of the best destinations in London to go shopping. You'll find Selfridges here, as well as John Lewis and Debenhams, all scattered through a variety of high street stores. Some of the biggest well-known brands here include Primark, Topshop, and Next. The closest tube to Oxford Street is Oxford Circus or Bond Street.

Regent Street and Jermyn Street

Regent Street has long been a popular destination for those who want to splash the cash in a stylish setting. There is an abundance of mid-range shops alongside some of the most iconic brands, including the Apple Store and Hamleys. Jermyn Street is not far from here, and has a reputation for men's clothing and fashion. Iconic shops here include Benson and

Clegg, and John Lobb. The closest tube stations to Regent Street are Piccadilly Circus and Oxford Circus.

Bond Street and Mayfair

If you have the urge to splash the cash then head to Bond Street and Mayfair. Here, you will find all the top designers and luxury goods that you can take back home with you. Bond Street and Mayfair have long been the playground for the rich, and it's not improbable to see a celebrity shopping at the local Burberry and Louis Vuitton stores here. The closest tube stations here are Piccadilly Circus and Bond Street Stations.

Westfield

There are two Westfield Centers in London – one at Stratford and the other at White City but both feature a variety of the best high street stores, including Next, Debenhams and Marks and Spencers, along with a number of designer stores, including Louis Vuitton and Jimmy Choo. Not only can you go shopping here, but there are other entertainment venues to enjoy. Take in a meal at one of the many restaurants here, enjoy a drink at one of the many bars or go and watch a movie at the cinema. The Westfield Stratford Center boasts over 250 shops. The closest tube station for Westfield White City is at White City Station; for Westfield Stratford Westfield it is Stratford Station.

Carnaby Street

During the swinging 60s, Canaby Street bloomed into life, becoming the fashion center of the United Kingdom. Carnaby is made up of 13 streets situated between Oxford and Regent Streets, boasting over 150 stores and fifty restaurants and bars to enjoy. It's a mixture of historical buildings, even older brands and contemporary names. The closest tube stations are Oxford Circus and Piccadilly Circus.

Covent Garden

Covent Garden is the ideal place to go if you are after fashionwear, handmade sweet treats and jewelry. It's also the best place to head for if you want something a little different, with a number of arts and craftworks at the Covent Garden Market. The closest tube station is located at Covent Garden.

King's Road

Located within stylish and sophisticated Chelsea, King's Road is a beautiful mixture of designer brands, exclusive stores, boutiques and high street brands, all with a scattering of restaurants and eateries in-between. It's especially popular with those who enjoy interior decorating, with Peter Jones and Heal's located here. For those who love the store Zara, one of the biggest stores is located close by. The Chelsea Antiques Market is located here. The closest tube station is Sloane Square.

Savile Row

For a long time, Savile Row has been synonymous with British dressmaking. You can still have a hand-made suit, all created in the traditional way, made here but it does come with a matching price tag. Henry Pool and Co., known as the first tailors on Savile Row, still operate here, as well as Ozwald Boateng. The closest tube stations to Savile Row are Bond Street and Piccadilly Circus.

Camden

If you're searching for the unusual, for something completely different when it comes to fashion, then don't look any further than Camden. For years, Camden has been famous for its quirky stores selling a range of fantastically different clothing and other items. Love punk? You'll find it here? Love Gothic clothing? Camden has it, too, as well as a range of body piercing and tattoo shops. Head up to the Camden Lock Market, where you can purchase a smorgasbord of items from vintage accessories to clothing that looks as though it did the time warp. The closest tube station is Camden Town.

Notting Hill

Made famous in recent years due to the blockbuster movie, *Notting Hill*, the real life version is a stylish area where you can discover a variety of one of a kind stores selling vintage clothes and accessories, antique stores, book shops and everything else in-between. The world famous Portobello Road Market is close by, featuring a wonderfully eclectic mixture of goods. For those wanting a little more sophistication, head to Westbourne Grove where you'll also find chic cafes and inspirational art galleries. The closest tube stations are Notting Hill Gate and Westbourne Park.

Spitalfields

With so many shopping areas featuring the same brands – both luxury and mid-range – it's quite nice to find something a little more independent. Spitalfields is certainly that. It's a wonderful stylish area where many young designers set up their shops with an equally brilliant atmosphere. But don't worry, there's a number of well-known brands to be found here, including Belstaff. For antiques and delicious food, head to the Old Spitalfields Market. The closest tube station is Liverpool Street.

Canary Wharf

Canary Wharf, located in the heart of London's Docklands, is where you will discover countless well-known businesses, but it's also home to a wide range of shops and shopping centers. There are actually five centers featuring over 120 stores amongst them, which includes high street and luxury names. It does get a little busy during the lunch hour, but otherwise it's a sleek and atmospheric place to shop. The closest tube station is Canary Wharf.

Chapter 12: The Best Times To Visit London

Summer sightseeing

London summers are relatively mild, with temperatures being in the region of 64 degrees Fahrenheit. There will be rare spikes, reaching to the 80s at times, but this is rare. This is pretty much the busiest time in London, with regard to tourism, and will be a great time to explore the different places that are attraction sites. Since rain is always a probability (London is in the UK after all), carrying an umbrella along will be a good idea.

Proms

The BBC proms, which are eight-week festivals chock-full with classical music, happen in both the Autumn and Summer seasons. These concerts, which are held on a daily basis at the Royal Albert Hall, start in the middle of July and last all the way until the second Saturday of September. The BBC symphony will perform the bulk of the concerts, but there will be guest orchestras that play throughout this 8-week period as well. One of these peripheral activities is the "Proms in the Parks", which is a late night celebration held outside the Royal Albert Hall for those who are unable to get tickets to the hall.

Autumn

By the time, the cooler months of London set in, vacations are usually over, at least on a large scale. At this time, children are going back to school. For the tourist who is flexible enough to plan his trip at this time, and who does not have an aversion to chilly weather, Autumn will mean lower air fares and hotel charges. You will have the chance to take part in the early September celebrations, which come complete with costumes, fireworks, and bonfires.

Winter

The winters are cold, miserable and damp. However, the city of London puts out a festive display for those guests who arrive for the Christmas holidays. There is Santa Land, where the kids will have a chance to chew the fat with Santa as well as Winter Wonderland, where ice skating is offered. The event will last until a week after New Year.

Circumstance and Pomp

Regardless of the season, state affairs, traditions, and events that attract tourists to London, varied events, such as the Royal wedding and Diamond Jubilee festivities will draw in crowds regardless of whatever season it is. The very highly ceremonial parliamentary opening that takes place every year is accompanied by the loud arrival (at least with regard to imagery) of the Queen and entourage in carriages and horseback. The Counting Of The Swans is yet another event that draws in quite the amount of tourists. Royal swans along the Thames are collected, inspected for injury or disease, and then released. This is pretty much a festive ceremony and you can view it from the riverbanks.

Chapter 13: Fun: Nightlife In London

The bar scene

The bulk of pubs in London close at around 11 pm, though if the pub has 24 hour licensing, it is allowed to run without closure. There are those pubs that have stuck to the traditional 11 pm closing time but chain pubs, bars, and clubs tend to push all the way to 1.30 am on weekdays. During weekends, they will close at around 3 am or 4 am. Some will stay open until around 7 am or 8 am, but will then open at a later hour than most of the others.

All around the city, you will find pubs with some of the weirdest names you will ever hear. In the states, you will not come across a pub called "The Dog and Duck". In London, this kind of naming is pretty much the norm.

For those tourists who are primarily interested in the up-market pubs for the rich folk, consider going to South Kensington or even Walton Street.

The Club Scene

Finding a decent club is not going to be difficult at all. This is especially so if you understand exactly what you are looking for. The great thing about London, with regard to clubbing, is that every area has a significantly different vibe from the next. This should help you look for and find your club of choice. While there will be clubs that only play one kind of music, you will find that there are clubs that devote every single night to a different theme. Check with the local bible before heading off and clubbing. Since this guide cannot cover everything, perhaps giving a few Club directories will help you get something that suits your style. Here are a few of them:

Timeout.com
VisitLondon.com
Skiddle.com

Clubbing in London may well get a little expensive but provided you arrive there early, you will at least save some money on things like cover charges. It is usually cheaper before 10 pm.

The Live Music Scene

Several places in the city are popular for their quality of music. For example, a jazz fan will have the time of his life at Ronnie Scott's, in Soho while the lovers of Rock will have themselves rocked at the Hammersmith Apollo. The Classical music group will find what they are looking for at the Royal Albert Hall.

What makes London unique, however, is the array of venues that organize concerts, both on a daily and weekly basis. You will not be short of a place to go.

Important tip: When traveling back to your hotel, make sure that the minicab you are traveling in is licensed. The minicab should have a sticker on the back window with the PCO number. If you are unsure of the cab's licensing, simply opt for another one.

Note: Smoking is banned in all UK restaurants and pubs.

Historic Pubs

Beer has always featured in London's history. As one of the most popular drinks of all time, there's certainly enough watering holes in the city where you enjoy a pint (or two). However, with all the shiny new nightclubs and the fancy cocktail bars scattered across London, sometimes you want to savour the history of the city, in addition to the drinks themselves. Read on to discover some of the best historic pubs in London.

The Grapes

Founded in 1583, The Grapes used to hold a reputation as the local hangout for numerous shady individuals – murderers and thieves included – where they could relieve patrons of their items before dumping the bodies into the murky depths of the river. Today, however, it's a pleasant place to enjoy a few drinks.

The Spaniards Inn

Located in Hampstead and founded in 1585, The Spaniards Inn was once mentioned by Dickens in his *Pickwick Papers*, and was immortalized in Bram Stoker's *Dracula*. If that wasn't enough, Byron and Keats used to drink here. Will you find inspiration here too?

The Old Bell Tavern

The Old Bell Tavern was founded in 1670, and was previously known as The Swan. When the Great Fire of London destroyed this place, Sir Christopher Wren had it restored so that the masons, who were building St. Bride's Church not far away, could come here and relax. Today, it features a variety of drinks but still retains the antique stained-glass windows from centuries ago.

Lamb and Flag

Founded in 1772, Lamb and Flag may be one of the smallest pubs you'll come across in London, but it certainly makes a big impression. It used to called *The Bucket of Blood*, due to the numerous brawls that continually occurred. However, those who drink here today usually keep their fists to themselves and the drinks flow.

The Olde Mitre

The Olde Mitre pub is located in Holborn and was founded in 1546. Even know, you can really feel as though you've stepped back to Tudor times. It's a quiet place, perfect for those seeking solitude and relaxation. Soak up the atmosphere while enjoying a range of beers, ales and wines.

The George Inn

The George Inn was founded in 1677 and used to be a coffee house that was frequented by Charles Dickens. It's a wonderful work of architecture and is actually one of the few terraced pubs still existing. Head inside, you'll see evidence of its days when it was a coach inn, as well as items from other periods, through portraits and tapestries.

Cittie of Yorke

The Cittie of Yorke pub has been tradition since 1645 and once inside, you'll find it to be a stunning collection of designs and features. The wooden beam ceiling certainly exude a historical feel, the roaring fireplaces give it a touch of distinction and coziness and the high ceilings make the place feel large and airy. With great drinks and a friend ambience, it's definitely a good place to visit.

Chapter 14: How Much It May Cost (For Low, Mid Range & High End)

As a London tourist, you will fall into the budget category, midrange category or top end category. As you may well predict, the cost and expenditure will vary greatly depending on the category you want to identify yourself as. Here are the likely costs you are likely to expect in all 3 tourist classes.

The Budget Tourist

As a budget tourist, you will likely find that dorm beds will offer you the least, with regard to expenditure. A dorm bed will cost 10 to 32 pounds.

Your lunch, if you opt to stick with Market-stall lunch will cost 5 pounds per meal. A supermarket sandwich will cost in the region of 5 pounds.

You will want to visit the many museums around London. The good news here is that most of them are free and will cost nothing especially if you have The London Pass.

Purchasing a stand by theatre ticket will cost 25 pounds, give or take.

For travel, you will want to avoid buses, trains and the like and travel by bike. Santander Cycles have a daily rental fee of 3 pounds.

Total cost: about 87 pounds.

The Midrange Tourist

As a midrange tourist, you may opt for a double room that will cost between 100 pounds to 160 pounds.

A decent dinner, such as a two-course meal accompanied by a glass of fine wine will cost around 40 pounds.

You will want to visit as many London Museums as possible. The good news here is that most of them are free and will cost nothing especially when you have the London Pass.

A theatre ticket will set you back anything between 20 pounds and 80 pounds.

The total combined costs sum up to around 200 pounds.

The Top end Tourist

The top end tourist will easily afford a four star or even a boutique hotel room. This one will cost around 250 Pounds.

Dinner will be nothing less than a three-course dinner in one of the top eateries along with a glass of wine. This will likely cost around 120 pounds.

A black cab trip will likely cost around 40 pounds.

A top theatre ticket will cost a minimum of 80 pounds.

Combined costs: Anything from 250 pounds to 1000 pounds

Tipping

Hotels - You will pay the porter around 2 pounds per bag. Gratuity for the room staff is however at your discretion.

Pubs - Unless table service is provided, tipping is really not expected. 2 pounds per round will be sufficient.

Restaurants- Often, service charge will be part of the bill. If it is not, then 10% should be given for decent service and up to 15% for exceptional service.

Taxis- There will be no need to go overboard with this. Just round the fare to the nearest pound and be done with it.

Chapter 15: Basic Survival Guide To Use In London

Currency & Exchange rates

The British pound, aka the Sterling Pound, is the official currency of the United Kingdom. The currency rankings show that the most popular pound exchange rate is the Euro to the GBP rate. The second most popular rate, perhaps to no surprise at all, is the USD (United States Dollar) to the GBP rate. The GBP is more valuable than the USD, with 1 GBP going for roughly 1.25 US dollars (November 16th 2016).

Language

The English language is the language spoken in London. It is vastly similar to American English, which only makes sense since American English was born from British English. However, there is a difference in accents, with the British accent differing from the American one. In London, you will have a problem getting through to the people there, as opposed to when you move away from London where the accents get considerably thicker. A good example of considerably thick accents is the Cockney accent. There are also some variations in spelling, with words like center being spelled as centre and meter, metre.

Emergency telephone numbers

In case you are in an accident or an emergency, it will be vital to know whom to call as well as the exact words to say.

Usually, the appropriate number to call will depend on whether the emergency is a life threatening injury, a fire or even an illness.

Here are some telephone numbers in London that you can call. All will charge nothing to place a call.

Non-emergency injuries may be treated at a GP surgery or even a local minor injuries unit.

Police, Fire, Ambulance, Coast guard: Tel 999, Tel 112

Crime (non-emergency): Tel 101

The clearer you come across to the relevant authorities, the more able they will be to help you. It is thus important to be concise and clear once you place your call and to be as direct as possible.

Help lines in London

Alcoholics Anonymous: 0845 769 7555

Child line (Help line specifically for children): 0800 1111

UK National Domestic Violence Help line: 0808 2000 247

Samaritans (For the depressed and suicidal): 084 5790 9090

Conclusion

"You will find no man, no intellectual who holds the will to leave London. No sir, when a man becomes tired of London, then it so goes that he is tired of life itself; for London holds all that life is able to afford."
Samuel Johnson.

London is a phenomenal place to visit. The culture and history there is nothing short of phenomenal. Indeed, you can never get tired of London- the food is great, the people are different and eager to help a stranger and it may well be the only place that makes a rainy night look and feel fashionable.

You would likely need an entire lifetime to completely exhaust all that London has to offer, especially given that it goes such a long way back. However, there is no need to feel low; whatever you manage to take from the city will enrich your life greatly in all ways.

Once again thank you for choosing *Lost Travelers*!

I hope we were able to provide you with the best travel tips when visiting London.

And we hope you enjoy your travels.

"Travel Brings Power and Love Back To Your Life"

\- Rumi

Finally, if you enjoyed this guide, then I'd like to ask you for a favor, would you be kind enough to leave a review for this book on Amazon? It'd be greatly appreciated!

- Simply search the keywords "London Lost Travelers" on Amazon or go to our Author page "Lost Travelers" to review.

Please know that your satisfaction is important to us. If you were not happy with the book, please email us with the reason so we may serve you more accordingly next time.

- Email: info@losttravelers.com

Thank you and good luck!

NOTES

NOTES

NOTES

NOTES

Preview Of 'New Zealand: The Ultimate New Zealand Travel Guide By A Traveler For A Traveler

Located 2,012 km to the south of Australia is New Zealand. There are two main islands comprising it, the North and South islands, and outlying islands scattered within the vicinity. Its two main islands are separated by a body of water known as the Cook Strait. The North Island is 829 km long. Its southern end is volcanic and because of this, there are plenty of excellent hot springs and geysers in the area. On the South island, lies the Southern Alps by the west end. Here is where one will find the highest point in New Zealand which is Mount Cook. It is 12,316 feet tall!

Some of the outlying islands are inhabited while others are not. The inhabited islands include Chatham, Great Barrier, and Stewart islands. The largest of the uninhabited islands are Campbell, Kermadec, Antipodes, and Auckland islands.

The first inhabitants of New Zealand were the Maoris. Their initial population was only 1,000 people. According to their oral history, it took the initial Maori population seven canoes to reach New Zealand from other parts of Polynesia. It was in the mid-1600s that the island cluster was explored by a man named Abel Tasma, a Dutch navigator. Another foreigner, a British by the name of James Cook, engaged in three voyages to New Zealand the first one taking place in 1769. New Zealand became a formal annex to Britain during the mid 1800s.

During this time, the Treaty of Waitangi was signed between Britain and the Maoris. It stated that there will be ample protection for Maori land should the Maoris accept British rule. Despite the treaty, tension between both factions intensified over time due to the continuous encroachment by British settlers.

Check out the rest of New Zealand: The Ultimate New Zealand Travel Guide on Amazon by simply searching it.

Check Out Our Other Books

Below you'll find some of our other popular books that are on Amazon and Kindle as well. Simply search the titles below to check them out. Alternatively, you can visit our author page (Lost Travelers) on Amazon to see other work done by us.

- Vienna: The Ultimate Vienna Travel Guide By A Traveler For A Traveler

- Barcelona: The Ultimate Barcelona Travel Guide By A Traveler For A Traveler

- London: The Ultimate London Travel Guide By A Traveler For A Traveler

- Istanbul: The Ultimate Istanbul Travel Guide By A Traveler For A Traveler

- Vietnam: The Ultimate Vietnam Travel Guide By A Traveler For A Traveler

- Peru: The Ultimate Peru Travel Guide By A Traveler For A Traveler

- Australia: The Ultimate Australia Guide By A Traveler For A Traveler

- Japan: The Ultimate Japan Travel Guide By A Traveler For A Traveler

- New Zealand: The Ultimate New Zealand Travel Guide By A Traveler For A Traveler

- Dublin: The Ultimate Dublin Travel Guide By A Traveler For A Traveler

- Thailand: The Ultimate Thailand Travel Guide By A Traveler For A Traveler

- Iceland: The Ultimate Iceland Travel Guide By A Traveler For A Traveler

- Santorini: The Ultimate Santorini Travel Guide By A Traveler For A Traveler

- Italy: The Ultimate Italy Travel Guide By A Traveler For A Traveler

You can simply search for these titles on the Amazon website to find them.

Made in the USA
San Bernardino, CA
22 January 2017